A History of Germs

MALARIA

 BY JIM OLLHOFF

Published by ABDO Publishing Company, 8000 West 78th Street, Suite 310, Edina, MN 55439. Copyright ©2010 by Abdo Consulting Group, Inc. International copyrights reserved in all countries. No part of this book may be reproduced in any form without written permission from the publisher. ABDO & Daughters™ is a trademark and logo of ABDO Publishing Company.

Printed in the United States.

 PRINTED ON RECYCLED PAPER

Editor: John Hamilton
Graphic Design: Sue Hamilton
Cover Design: John Hamilton
Cover Photo: iStock
Interior Photos and Illustrations: AP-pgs 6, 18, 24, & 28; Getty Images-pgs 4, 7, 9, & 17; iStockphoto-pgs 1, 3, 5, & 8; Mark Plonsky-pgs 15, 29, & 31; North Wind Picture Archives-pg 14; Nothing But Nets-pg 25; Peter Arnold Inc-pgs 12, 13, & 21; and Photo Researchers-pgs 10, 11, 19, 20, 23, & 27.

Library of Congress Cataloging-in-Publication Data

Ollhoff, Jim, 1959-
  Malaria / Jim Ollhof.
    p. cm. – (A history of germs)
  Includes index.
  ISBN 978-1-60453-500-6
  1. Malaria–Juvenile literature. I. Title.

QR201.M3O45 2010
616.9'362–dc22

                    2008055059

CONTENTS

MALARIA

In central Africa, a mother brings her son to the village doctor. The child is tired all the time, and has a high fever. The mother is afraid he is about to die. The doctor examines the child. "He has malaria," the doctor says. "But we have no medicine today. Here's an aspirin." The doctor hands her a pill. "Come back tomorrow, maybe we'll have the medicine then."

A Sudanese boy is comforted by his mother as he is treated for malaria.

When infected mosquitoes bite, they spread the parasite that causes malaria.

This terrible scenario is acted out thousands of times each day in Africa and the tropical areas of Southeast Asia and South America. Three hundred million people get malaria each year. One million die, most of them children less than five years old. Treatment and prevention are available, but in many areas of the world people simply can't get the medicines they need.

Malaria is caused by a parasite that is spread by mosquitoes. Mosquitoes live in swampy areas, or places with lots of standing water. Even before the discovery of the malaria microorganism, people knew that the disease occurred in tropical areas near swamps. They thought it was caused by the stale, putrid air of the swamps. In fact, the word malaria comes from an Italian phrase that means "bad air." But it is not the air in the swamps that causes the disease—it is the mosquitoes that live in the swamps. Mosquitoes pass along the malaria parasite when they bite people.

In many places, people simply can't get the medicine they need.

WHY IS A CURABLE DISEASE SO DEADLY?

If a person in North America or Europe contracts malaria, doctors can give them medication that will cure them. However, 90 percent of the world's cases of malaria happen in sub-Saharan Africa. Sub-Saharan means the area south of the Sahara Desert, in countries such as Chad, Mali, and Sierra Leone. There are also outbreaks of malaria in India, Central and South America, Southeast Asia, and other places. These places are hot most of the year, and have large amounts of standing water, which mosquitoes need to breed.

A huge body of standing water provides the perfect breeding ground for mosquitoes in Southeast Asia's country of Thailand.

Why is malaria such a terrible disease if a cure exists? The question can be partially answered by one word: money. Many of the areas in central Africa suffer from crushing poverty, and the medicines for malaria are very expensive. The best medicines are out of reach for many countries suffering from malaria. Only about 3 out of every 100 children with malaria get the medicine they need.

A mother waits at a health center in Ghana, Africa. Her son has been infected with malaria. His legs still show the mosquito bites. Only about 3 out of every 100 children with malaria get the medicine they need.

But the problem is not just that poverty-stricken people can't afford malaria medicines. The problem is also that malaria creates poverty. In some areas of sub-Saharan Africa, half of hospital and clinic admissions are because of malaria. Parents can't work when they have to stay home with a sick child. Farmers don't plant many crops because they know that during harvest time most people will be sick with malaria and can't work. Africa has many undeveloped markets, since traders don't want to travel to areas where there is malaria. The tourist industry is undeveloped. When children are sick, they can't go to school.

A hut and boat near standing water in Ethiopia. The area is a perfect breeding ground for mosquitoes.

When people can barely afford to feed themselves, they spend their wages on food instead of housing and farms. Mosquitoes can get inside flimsily built houses. Inadequate farms have land with standing water and weeds that create breeding grounds for mosquitoes.

Further, desperately poor people are usually undernourished. This makes them more susceptible to malaria. When more people have malaria, the mosquitoes bite more people and pass the parasite on. This results in epidemics that can wreak havoc on whole villages.

The economic effects of malaria are massive, but the human pain is even greater. Children and pregnant women are at greatest risk. The loss of a child or a mother is devastating to a family. Even if a child survives malaria, permanent brain damage may result from the disease. A child dies from malaria every 30 seconds. This horrific disease creates untold misery.

A father carries the cross for his two-year-old daughter's grave as other family members carry the coffin. The girl died from malaria in Burundi, Africa. A child dies from malaria every 30 seconds.

WHAT IS MALARIA?

Malaria is caused by a parasite that gets into the body and reproduces. There are actually several types of microorganisms that cause malaria. The most deadly type is caused by the microorganism called *plasmodium falciparum*. This type is responsible for 90 percent of malaria deaths.

The mosquito that carries the malaria parasite is the *anopheles* mosquito. The process of malaria starts when a mosquito feeds on a person who already has the disease. The malaria parasite gets into the mosquito. There, the *plasmodium falciparum* send tiny cells into the saliva glands of the mosquito. The mosquito is now infected with malaria.

The *anopheles* mosquito often carries the malaria parasite.

Next, the infected mosquito feeds on a malaria-free person. As the mosquito bites, its saliva glands inject the malaria parasite into the bloodstream of the victim.

From there, the bloodstream carries the parasite through the person's body. Within minutes of the mosquito bite, the parasite enters the victim's liver. It infects the liver so fast that the person's immune system cannot respond to the invader. Once the parasite is inside the liver cells, it safely hides from the person's powerful immune system. The immune system won't attack its own liver cells.

Malaria is caused by *plasmodium* parasites. They enter the blood after a bite (upper left) from an infected *anopheles* mosquito, and travel (red arrows) through the blood to the liver (brown, lower center). Here, they multiply and invade red blood cells, causing the cells to swell and burst. The lack of red blood cells leads to anemia, and the presence of plasmodia in the blood causes a fever. Some plasmodia invade more red blood cells, and others are taken up by other mosquitoes (upper right), continuing the cycle.

The parasite stays safely hidden in the liver, where it lives for about two weeks. The parasite matures and reproduces by the thousands. The person experiences no symptoms during this time.

Then, the parasites burst out of the liver and back into the bloodstream, where they burrow into red blood cells. Once again, the parasite is safe from the immune system, because the immune system won't attack its own red blood cells.

Once inside a red blood cell, the parasite reproduces again. When there are enough parasites in the red blood cell, the cell bursts. This destroys the cell and releases new parasites into the bloodstream. Blood cells, which carry oxygen to the body's tissues, are bursting all over, releasing new parasites. The body's immune system is overwhelmed. The immune system is caught off guard by the sudden onslaught of invaders.

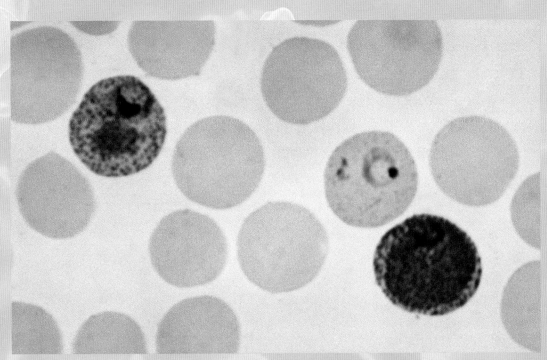

Plasmodium parasites have infected three red blood cells. Chills and fever are experienced by the victim when the red blood cells burst.

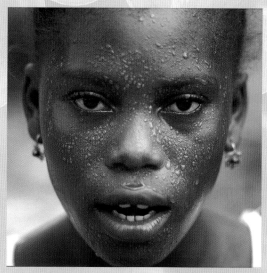

Malaria victims experience high fever, chills, and severe headaches.

The infected person experiences a high fever and chills. The person becomes listless, with a severe headache. The spleen, which is responsible for cleaning up damaged blood cells, becomes overwhelmed and enlarged. The infected blood cells become sticky, and often clog up the small blood vessels. If the small blood vessels in the brain get clogged, the person can experience convulsions, coma, and death.

Next, an uninfected mosquito feeds on the sick person. The mosquito takes the parasite into its body, and the process starts all over again.

In some diseases, like influenza or smallpox, once a person gets the disease, they probably won't ever get it again. This is called immunity. Immunity happens because the person's immune system "remembers" how to fight a disease. But with malaria, the body never develops immunity. People are often infected every year. With repeated infections, a person will often not get the disease as severely. This is why more children than adults die of malaria. But the cycle of malaria depends on the breeding cycle of the mosquitoes, and that cycle happens every year.

With malaria, the body never develops immunity.

A BRIEF HISTORY OF MALARIA

Malaria has probably been around for millions of years. The earliest records of the disease are from ancient Chinese medical writings, dating back to 2700 BC. They describe swampy areas where people suffered from fevers, pain, and sometimes death. These symptoms closely resemble malaria. The ancient Egyptians also had trouble with malaria. Egyptian mummies have been found that have enlarged spleens, one of the characteristic signs of the disease.

Malaria was recognized in ancient Greece. The Greeks talked about the decline of some city-states because of an illness that was probably malaria. Some historians believe that the Greek King Alexander the Great died of malaria in 323 BC.

Ancient Indian Sanskrit writings described malaria and suggested it was from the bites of insects. Roman writers attributed the disease to swamps.

Some believe that Alexander the Great, king of Macedon and conqueror of Greece, Egypt, and Persia, may have died of malaria at the age of 32.

Without realizing it, the Europeans made Africa's problem with malaria much worse. Before the arrival of the British and other Europeans, Africans had less of a problem with malaria. Many African tribes lived in higher altitudes, higher than where mosquitoes live. The tribes also lived in small bands, so if malaria attacked one tribe, there was only a small group of people infected. Widespread epidemics were rare.

However, when the Europeans entered Africa in the 1800s, they brought with them their understanding of how to live. The Europeans moved close to the rivers and swampy areas where there would be plenty of water for crops. They created cities. Where cities grow, standing water is everywhere—places where mosquitoes can breed. Further, when people live close to each other in cities, there is ripe opportunity for quick-spreading epidemics.

In large cities there is often a lot of standing water. This is the perfect breeding ground for mosquitoes. An increase in the mosquito population, in turn, causes an increase in malaria.

Charles Louis Alphonse Laveran, a French military doctor, discovered the parasite in the blood of malaria victims. He was awarded the Nobel Prize for his work in 1907.

In 1945, an American soldier sprays a swampy area to kill mosquito larvae.

In 1880, a French military doctor named Charles Louis Alphonse Laveran discovered the parasite in the blood of malaria victims. For his discovery, he was awarded the Nobel Prize a few years later. In 1897 and 1898, British and Italian doctors showed that mosquitoes transmitted the virus to humans.

In the early 1900s, the United States and European countries began trying to control mosquito breeding. Insecticides were sprayed heavily in high-risk areas. After World War II, scientists invented an insecticide called DDT. This was sprayed heavily, greatly reducing the mosquito population. Later, biologists discovered that DDT had many negative effects, and so its use was discontinued in the United States. But, it helped to snuff out the *anopheles* mosquito. By 1951, North America and Europe were mostly malaria-free.

TREATMENTS AND CURES FOR MALARIA ☣

A vaccine is a drug that gives people immunity to a disease. This means that a person who gets a vaccination for malaria would never contract malaria again.

For thousands of years, the disease smallpox killed millions of people each year. Edward Jenner created a vaccine in 1796. It took a long time, but aggressive vaccination programs and lightning-fast responses to smallpox outbreaks made the

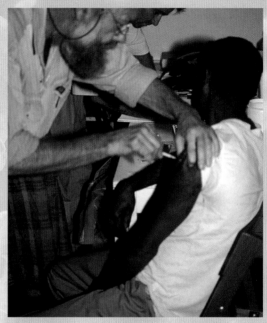

A man is given an experimental malaria vaccine.

disease weaker and weaker. By 1980, scientists declared smallpox wiped off the face of the earth—no one will ever get smallpox again.

Scientists hope that malaria will suffer the same fate as smallpox. But right now, doctors don't have a vaccine. Doctors have treatments that will kill the parasite. Doctors also have drugs that can prevent malaria. A preventative drug keeps people from getting the disease as long as they take the medicine. That's different from a vaccine. With a vaccine, one dose gives people a permanent immunity.

Treatments were used long before doctors understood the cause of the disease. In China, doctors had an effective treatment for malaria in about 200 BC. They used the leaves of the qinghao plant (or wormwood) to develop an effective treatment. In the 1970s, Chinese scientists isolated the active ingredient in the plant. It is now made into the drug artemisinin, one of the most effective medicines to combat malaria.

The leaves of the qinghao plant (or wormwood) were used by ancient Chinese herbalists to treat malaria. Now it is harvested as a source of the anti-malaria drug artemisinin.

Men harvest bark from cinchona trees in South America. The bark of these trees contains high levels of quinine, a strong antimalarial drug. Cinchona bark was the first source of this drug. During harvesting, the outer bark is removed, exposing the inner bark. After being cleaned, the inner bark is stripped from the tree with a knife, stacked, and dried in the sun.

In South America, malaria victims chewed the bark of the cinchona tree. Spanish explorers discovered its use when they first landed in Central and South America. They called it Peruvian bark. They took it back to Europe, where people used it as an effective treatment. Today, we call the medicine quinine. It has been used for hundreds of years in Europe and the United States.

Cinchona bark was chewed as a treatment for malaria.

Other drugs became available for treatments of malaria. People began to hope that the medications could get rid of malaria. However, a disturbing setback occurred in the 1970s and 1980s. Malaria became resistant to some of the medications. The drugs became less and less effective as the parasite changed. Malaria had been on the decline. But with the emergence of drug-resistant parasites, malaria increased again.

Scientists continue experimenting with new and more effective drugs. The most effective medicines are combinations of two or more drugs. The combination, or cocktail, makes it more difficult for the parasite to develop a resistance.

CONTROL OF MALARIA

In many African countries, malaria is out of control. Malaria can't be controlled with just one drug or one insecticide. It can't be controlled with one strategy. Controlling malaria requires several strategies that must be performed simultaneously.

Insecticide-treated mosquito nets are an important part of controlling malaria. Mosquitoes mostly feed at night, and if people sleep under mosquito netting, the chances of contracting malaria are greatly reduced. However, most of the nets are sitting in warehouses because the people can't afford the $2 to pay for them. Approximately less than 10 percent of the people who need a net actually have one.

Insecticide is another important way to help. Killing mosquitoes is a quick way to put a dent in how the malaria parasite is transmitted. But if engineers spray enough chemicals to kill every mosquito, people get sick and die from the chemicals. Further, mosquitoes become resistant to insecticide.

Controlling malaria requires several strategies that must be performed simultaneously.

Mosquitoes mostly feed at night. If people sleep under mosquito netting, the chances of contracting malaria are greatly reduced. However, approximately less than 10 percent of the people who need a net actually have one. Global efforts are underway to get nets in the hands of the people who need them.

At one time, DDT was an effective mosquito-killing weapon. But today, mosquitoes have evolved that are no longer affected by DDT.

Another important approach to controlling malaria is to make sure the land does not have standing water, which creates breeding areas for mosquitoes. Garbage dumps are prime places for mosquitoes to breed. Even old tires that lie around can fill with water.

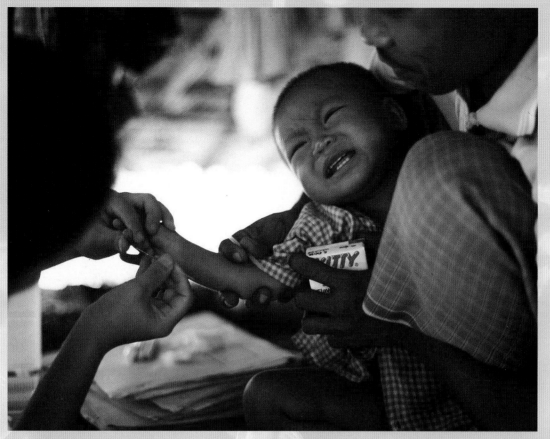

A young boy is tested for malaria in a refugee camp. In remote areas or places torn by civil war, there is little or no medical help for malaria victims.

Access to medical services is something most people take for granted in the developed world. But in rural areas in many African countries, people have little or no access to clinics or hospitals. Some places are torn by civil war, and so there is no medical access. Some villages are very remote and there are no roads. Many villages have no doctors, only people who once worked with a doctor, or even people with no medical training at all—they just want to help. It is necessary to have clinics, doctors, and local governments organized and ready. All these pieces are called infrastructure, which is an absolute necessity in order to fight malaria.

A related issue is that many people who can seek medical help refuse to see a doctor. Some people don't trust western medicine. Some people migrate to other places because of famine or war. Some people are afraid to travel through dangerous areas. In places where no telephones or televisions exist, it is often difficult to let people know when hospitals or clinics set up. Local community organizers are needed to spread the word.

Nothing But Nets is an organization that provides mosquito netting for free.

Obviously, one of the most important steps in controlling malaria is getting medicines. There are medicines available, but the least expensive medicines are often the least effective. The malaria parasite has become resistant to some of the medicines. Less than three percent of children with malaria receive the most effective medicines. A lot of money is needed to pay for more-effective medicines and get them to the children who need them.

Malaria deaths go down when money is available to do these things. However, funding is often difficult to find. Sometimes a foundation or corporation will donate money, but when the money is used up, malaria deaths go up again.

Malaria deaths go down when there is money. When money is used up, deaths go up again.

A COMING MALARIA VACCINE?

This is an exciting time for scientists who study malaria. Many believe they are on the verge of finding a vaccine for malaria.

There are many reasons why a malaria vaccination has been slow in coming. One reason is the parasite itself. The malaria parasite has a whole life cycle inside the human body, so it constantly changes. It's difficult for the immune system to deal with an invader that is constantly changing. Further, the parasite hides within the cells of the human body, making it difficult for the immune system to find it.

Perhaps the biggest reason why malaria vaccination has been slow is the lack of funding. It takes years to develop a vaccine, and years of testing. It is a very expensive process. Since malaria no longer exists in richer countries, it has been difficult to find funding. There aren't enough people speaking up about malaria, so politicians and government officials don't set aside much money for it.

Scientists are currently working on a number of different kinds of vaccines. The different drugs work to stop malaria in different ways.

Are we on the verge of finding a malaria vaccine?

Bill Gates, chairman of Microsoft Corporation and co-chair of the Bill and Melinda Gates Foundation, gave nearly $168 million to research a new generation of malaria vaccines in 2008.

One kind of vaccine works to block the parasite from entering human blood cells. Another possible vaccine prevents the young parasite from growing into an adult parasite, thus making it unable to reproduce. A third kind of vaccine boosts the body's ability to make antibodies to combat the parasite. Another drug boosts the immune system of the *mosquito*, making the insect resistant to the parasite.

All of these drugs are currently in development. It's doubtful that all of them will work, but scientists hope that at least one will work as a vaccine. Scientists hope, but can't guarantee, that a vaccine will be ready in a few years.

People frequently hope that huge problems will be solved with a big scientific breakthrough. Few scientists, however, think that a single vaccine will solve the malaria problem. It will still take insecticides, draining swampy areas, local community support and infrastructure, and above all, funding, to make a vaccine work.

Still, a vaccine could go a long way in combating such a terrible disease. Eradicating malaria will be difficult—but it is certainly possible.

A mosquito feeds on a human host. People hope a scientific breakthrough will stop the parasites that mosquitoes carry from being transmitted from one malaria victim to the next.

Eradicating malaria will be difficult—but it is certainly possible.

GLOSSARY

ANOPHELES MOSQUITO

The type of mosquito that carries the malaria parasite. They live in tropical areas, and breed wherever they can find standing water.

EPIDEMIC

A disease that quickly spreads across a population or a large area.

INFRASTRUCTURE

Everything that makes up the basic facilities of a region. This includes bridges, roads, communication systems, transportation systems, and community involvement.

INSECTICIDE

Any chemical that kills insects. In the case of malaria, insecticide is needed to kill the mosquitoes that spread the disease.

MICROORGANISM

A tiny organism, only visible under a microscope.

PARASITE

Any plant or animal that lives in or on another organism, usually in a way that harms the host. In the case of malaria, the microorganism lives inside the human body, and is often deadly.

Plasmodium falciparum

The scientific name of the most deadly of the malaria parasites.

Sub-Sahara

The area of Africa that is south of the Sahara desert.

Vaccine

A drug that gives the recipient immunity to a disease. A vaccine does not currently exist for malaria, but several possible vaccines are in development.

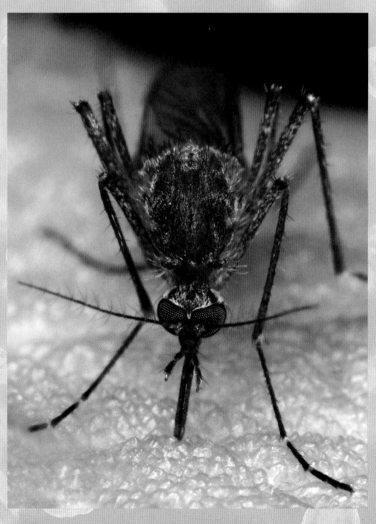

Can malaria be stopped? Many people are trying to make that happen.

INDEX